THE POCKET GUIDE TO

SEASONAL

LARGEMOUTH BASS

PATTERNS

THE POCKET GUIDE TO

SEASONAL

LARGEMOUTH BASS

PATTERNS

AN ANGLER'S QUICK REFERENCE BOOK

MONTE BURCH

Skyhorse Publishing

Skyhorse Publishing books may be purchased in bulk at special discounts for sales promotion, corporate gifts, fund-raising, or educational purposes. Special editions can also be created to specifications. For details, contact the Special Sales Department, Skyhorse Publishing, 307 West 36th Street, 11th Floor, New York, NY 10018 or info@skyhorsepublishing.com.

Skyhorse® and Skyhorse Publishing® are registered trademarks of Skyhorse Publishing, Inc.®, a Delaware corporation.

Visit our website at www.skyhorsepublishing.com.

10 9 8 7 6

Library of Congress Cataloging-in-Publication Data is available on file.

Cover design by Tom Lau
Cover illustration: iStockphoto/Vasiliy Voropaev

Print ISBN: 978-1-63450-810-0
Ebook ISBN: 978-1-63450-819-3

Printed in China

CONTENTS

The extremely popular black bass family, from the genus *Micropterus*, are actually members of the sunfish family. They include the most popular game fishes in America: the largemouth, smallmouth (often called brown bass), and spotted or Kentucky bass, as well as lesser known cousins like the Redeye, Guadalupe, and Suwannee bass.

The pugnacious attitude of the bass family is one of the reasons for their popularity. The habits of sunfishes are fairly similar. They are ambushers waiting in submerged cover for their prey. Primarily sight and sound feeders, they'll readily attack almost anything that moves, including the thousands of lures that have been designed just for these popular species.

Probably the main popularity of the black basses, however, is their wide distribution across the country and in a variety of different waters. They have been transplanted and spread far from their native ranges, from north to south, east to west. Almost anyone in the United States can find some kind of bass fishing fairly close to home.

Black bass also attract anglers from all walks of life, from the cane pole fisherman with a minnow to the avid tournament angler with thousands of dollars in boat and equipment.

Successful bass fishing may be enjoyed throughout the year (in areas with open water) by understanding the seasonal habits of bass. Rather than continually casting the shorelines and hoping for bass, concentrate on locating bass-holding areas. These areas can vary with the seasons from shallow to deep water, as well as a wide variety of cover and structure. The key is to not only discover these areas, but also the migration routes between these holding areas.

This is called "patterning" the fish, or determining where the fish will be in a given lake, pond, reservoir, or even river at different times of the year, depending on several factors including: amount of daylight, water temperature, water clarity, water conditions, and so forth. The exact dates, including the length of the various patterns, will vary across the country, but the biological and seasonal patterns will remain the same.

The bass fishing year can be classified into eight specific seasonal periods: early spring, pre-spawn, spawn, post spawn, summer, early fall, late fall, and winter.

How to Use This Book

The illustrations in this book are based on a typical "good" bass fishing reservoir in the Midwest. Some southern lakes will have more shallow water and (usually) less clarity. Highland lakes, and the Great

Lakes will be deeper and have more clarity, as will many western reservoirs. Not all features will be found in all lakes, but those shown indicate the best locations for bass throughout the various seasons on that particular lake. Each of the eight different seasonal bass time patterns are described along with approximate water temperatures, clarity, and water conditions.

Typical locations of bass during each period is indicated on a drawing of the sample lake.

The best choice in lures and best tactics are also described for each of the patterns.

In addition, the following two pages contain a handy Quick Reference Chart with the information condensed and available for instant use.

The majority of the information concerns fishing for America's favorite fish, the large-

PERIOD	SURFACE TEMP	LURE	LOCATION
EARLY SPRING	45–54 DEGREES	1/4 TO 3/8 OZ. JIG WITH PORK, PLASTIC, OR LEATHER TRAILER IN BLACK OR BROWN. WEIGHTED SPINNERBAITS OR CRANKBAITS. TINY 1/8 TO 1/4 OZ. ROAD RUNNERS.	SOUTH FACING BANKS. UPPER ENDS OF RESERVOIR TRIBUTARIES, AREAS WITH MATERIAL IN THE WATER INCLUDING TURBIDITY, TIMBER, ROCKY SHOALS, SCATTERED BOULDERS.
PRE-SPAWN	55–65 DEGREES	SPINNERBAITS, CRANKBAITS, JERKBAITS, TOPWATERS, BUZZBAITS, AND LIPLESS RATTLING CRANKBAITS.	MIGRATION ROUTES BETWEEN DEEP WATER AND SPAWNING AREAS. SHALLOW FLATS CLOSE TO MAJOR CREEK CHANNELS. SHALLOW BAYS AND COVES.
SPAWN	67–75 DEGREES	PLASTIC WORMS, TUBE LURES, TOPWATER LURES. SINGLE BEST LURE IS PLASTIC SALAMANDER.	SHALLOW BAYS, COVES, ANO FLATS WITH PEA GRAVEL. CHUNK ROCK BANKS ARE ALSO GOOD.
POST SPAWN	75–80 DEGREES	PIG AND JIG, PLASTIC WORMS, GRUBS, AND TUBE LURES. CRANK-BAITS, LIPLESS RATTLING CRANKBAITS, AND SPINNERBAITS WILL HELP LOCATE BASS.	RETURN TO THE MIGRATION ROUTES BETWEEN SPAWNING AREAS AND DEEP WATER. KEY ON DEEPER ENDS OF MAIN LAKE POINTS AND CREEK CHANNELS.

PERIOD	SURFACE TEMP	LURE	LOCATION
SUMMER	80 DEGREES AND HIGHER	SHALLOW: TOPWATER, CRANKBAITS, SPINNER-BAITS. DEEP: PLASTIC WORMS, TUBE LURES, GRUBS, AND DEEP-RUNNING CRANKBAITS.	SHALLOW: WEEDS, MOSS, AND HEAVY COVER. DEEP: DEEP WATER STRUCTURE, HUMPS, AND ISLANDS
EARLY FALL	80–60 DEGREES	SPINNERBAITS, BUZZ-BAITS, CRANKBAITS, AND LIPLESS RATTLING CRANKS.	MAJOR TRIBUTARIES AND MIGRATION ROUTES BETWEEN DEEP AND SHALLOW AREAS.
LATE FALL	60–42 DEGREES	SPINNERBAITS, CRANK-BAITS, LIPLESS RATTLING CRANKBAITS, AND BUZZBAITS. LATER, PIG AND JIG.	SHALLOW FLATS, MAJOR TRIBUTARIES, CREEKS, MIGRATION ROUTES.
WINTER	45 DEGREES	PIG AND JIG, JIGS, JIGGING SPOONS, AND JERK BAITS.	BLUFFS, SUBMERGED TREES, DEEP CREEK CHANNELS.

mouth bass, but references are also made to specific tactics for the other species. Information on fishing rivers as well as strip or mining pits and ponds is also covered.

Tools

Today's bass anglers have a number of excellent tools. The most basic are hydrographical or lake maps. Compare your lake map with the illustrations of the hypothetical example lake and mark the locations of suggested prime fish-holding areas on your map, according to the seasonal patterns. For instance, you might wish to label early spring pattern locations with A, pre-spawn locations with B, and so forth. This will help eliminate unproductive water and give you an idea of where to start prospecting once you are on the water.

A sonar or depth finder, or "fish finder," is an invaluable tool for most bass anglers,

Topographical maps are invaluable for studying seasonal patterns.

except for those fishing small ponds and streams. Not only do today's sonars reveal structure, baitfish, and even bass, they also provide temperature information and hydrographical maps. And with GPS navigating as well, marking fishing-holding areas is an easy chore. Structure is an extremely important factor in bass fishing, but the single most important factor in determining bass patterns is knowing the water temperature.

Black bass are active according to the temperature of the water surrounding their cold-blooded bodies. The range for optimum bass activity is from 50 to 85 degrees F, with the mid-point, about 70 degrees F, the preferred temperature and the temperature at which most bass activity takes place. Largemouth bass spawn when the temperature reaches 62 to 65 degrees F in the spring. This doesn't mean, however, that bass won't move or feed in temperatures other than the most

Today's sonars make it easy to not only navigate, but to locate structure, bait, and bass, as well as determine water temperature.

comfortable. They must eat and will often move in and out of water extremes for short periods of time to feed, but they will return to those areas that are most comfortable to them. Their metabolism is such that less food is required in colder temperatures. The warmer the temperature becomes, the more food their metabolism requires, up to a point where the heat causes discomfort.

Bass will attempt to seek the zone of temperature that best suits them and will be found in different areas of the water at different times of the year, as well as different times of day or night according to the variance in water temperature. At times even a degree or two of water can create a "hot" spot. Learning how to correctly use sonar, maps, and temperature gauges can add greatly to black bass angling success. Another useful tool is a fishing log. Keeping track of temperatures, water conditions, time of year, time of day, moon phases, and successful fishing locations can also add to your success.

EARLY SPRING

Temperature: Lower 40s to 50 degrees F
Clarity: Normally clear
Water Conditions: Normally stable

Water temperatures at this time will range from 40 to 50 degrees F, depending on locality. Water clarity on lakes and reservoirs will normally run from clear to extremely clear, due to the lack of spring rains and runoff, although snow melt can be a factor in some northern areas.

This is a tough one, a time when it's hit or miss angling. Bass are beginning to move out of their winter pattern, but not established yet, so it's search-and-hunt with hit-or-miss angling. Some days you're going to get lucky, but most are going to be tough, more like musky fishing than bass angling.

Bass Locations

Bass will be found any place there is even a slight warming of the water. Key spots include the south facing banks of north and northwestern coves, creeks, and tributaries of most reservoirs and lakes. Upper ends of reservoir tributaries warm first, as well as those areas with more material in the water, including turbidity, standing timber, rocky shoals, scattered boulders, even boathouses or marina docks. Bass will, however, still be keyed to winter holding areas, but not as concentrated.

Look for deep water winter holding spots, then possible spawning areas nearby. Early spring bass will begin to locate along migration routes between these areas. As the day warms up they move shallow, often simply vertically rather than horizontally. When the temperature drops back down, they move back down into deeper water. Many pros start looking for them on the first major drop-offs between shallow and deep water. Good spots are bluffs, creek channels, channel

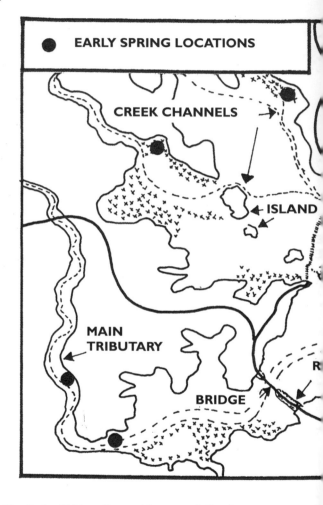

EARLY SPRING LOCATIONS

CREEK CHANNELS

ISLAND

MAIN
TRIBUTARY

BRIDGE

R

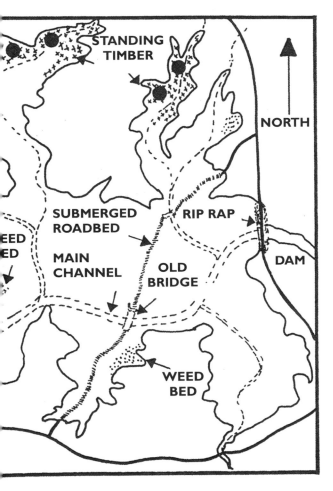

STANDING TIMBER

NORTH

SUBMERGED ROADBED

RIP RAP

DAM

MAIN CHANNEL

OLD BRIDGE

WEED BED

WEED BED

bends close to the bluffs, as well as deeper flats off creek channels.

The depth should be close to deep water, but with plenty of migration routes to follow. Look for bass anywhere from 8 to 30 feet deep.

Lure Choices

Lure choices are somewhat limited. One of my favorites for this time of the year is a jig with a pork or plastic trailer. One quarter to three ounces is the most common choice with black, brown, or colors with added streaks of red, blue, chartreuse, and so forth. Plastic crawdad trailers are especially good at this time of the year. Heavy spinnerbaits (slow rolled) are good, as are weighted spinnerbaits or crankbaits. These can be weighted by sliding a worm sinker over the line before tying on the lure. A toothpick pegs the weight ahead of the lure. Or, you can crimp on a

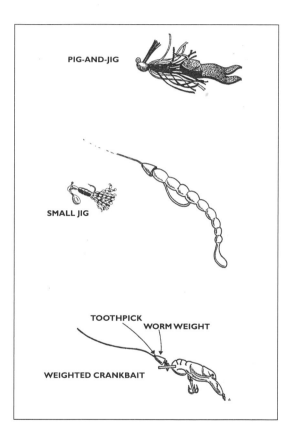

PIG-AND-JIG

SMALL JIG

TOOTHPICK

WORM WEIGHT

WEIGHTED CRANKBAIT

split shot, but you'll have more problems with hangups. Tiny ⅛- and ¼-ounce spinner jigs, such as Road Runners, can also be deadly. These tiny jigs should be fished very slowly, just off the edges of the creek channel drops.

Another deadly lure and tactic is using suspended jerkbaits. This is extremely effective in late winter as well as very early spring. Although standard jerkbaits will work, weighted versions are the most successful. Properly weighted jerkbaits will suspend and hover almost motionless when the retrieve is stopped. With a baitfish hovering right in front of their nose, even lethargic winter bass can be enticed, especially big bass. This tactic is especially good on clear lakes.

Weighted jerkbaits have been around for a long time, but few fishermen know about or use them. The most common weighting method of the past was to wind

Suspending jerkbaits are extremely productive in early spring.

pieces of wire solder around the center hook, adding or removing until the bait would suspend when pushed down in the water in your bathtub. Dedicated anglers then began drilling holes in the bottom of the bait and adding snips of solder or lead weights to achieve the same suspending qualities. Small stick-on dots were then produced to achieve the weightless action. A number of manufacturers now produce weighted jerkbaits, including some with rattles in them for added attraction.

Jerkbaits are most effective under certain conditions, usually after fronts and times when fish are inactive. They aren't as effective in muddy water and low visibility situations. Under these and cold water conditions, the longer you can keep a bait in front of the fish, the better your chances of getting him to come up and slash at it. The more it stays in the so-called strike zone, the better it is going to be. The trick is to work the bait really slow. Give it a sweeping motion, then stop, and maybe twitch it a couple of times. Fish it very slowly and let the bait sit suspended 10 to 15 seconds at a time. In most instances the bass are looking for dying or inactive shad, something that is very easy for them to eat.

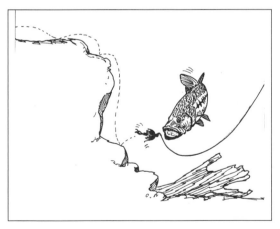

Pitching, flipping, and slowly bouncing a pig-and-jig or other type of jig is the most effective early spring tactic.

One of the most important factors is to work the jerkbait parallel to some type of cover, structure, drop-off, or weed line, keeping the bait in the strike zone as long as possible. It is also important to make sure no matter what depth zone you're fishing, the bait should be above the fish. It is easy to get bass to come up to take a bite, but it is hard to get them to go down. Actually, the jerkbait can be effective year-round under clear conditions. It is extremely good for fishing the Great Lakes for smallmouth, and even a jerkbait suspended two feet down can bring fish up from deep water.

Tactics

Bass are just starting to come out of their winter seasonal pattern. Their metabolism is extremely slow, and as a result they're usually slow to move, won't chase a lure far, nor make fast strikes at it. Regardless

Slow baits, such as a pig-and-jig, are good choices for early spring.

of the lure, make your retrieves as slow as you think possible, then slow down some more.

Best days to fish are those after a couple of days of warming weather. Right after a front comes through can be the toughest, but jerkbaits and flipping jigs into heavy protected cover can produce.

Fish through the middle of the day when the sun and heat is the highest, and look for the most sheltered spots that will have the warmest water.

Temperature: 50 to 65 degrees F
Clarity: Clear to muddy
Water Conditions: Often rising

Normally the water will run slightly warmer than early spring, although there may be occasional fronts that will drop the temperature lower. Look for water temperature between 55 and 65 degrees F. Clarity can change rapidly and can range from extremely clear to turbid due to incoming spring rains.

Regardless of the water you're fishing—sprawling reservoir, natural lake, river, community lake, or farm pond—the pre-spawn period provides the best opportunities for catching the biggest trophy bass. This is the time of year when you can hang the biggest bass of your life. This is also the time when anybody can catch a bass. But first you have to find them.

Bass Locations

As the water temperature continues to rise from early spring, bass begin an ongoing migration from their winter deep-water holding spots prior to spawning in the shallow bays, coves, and on the 45-degree sloping rubble or gravel banks.

Bass are more scattered now than any other time of the year and are continually roaming. Key locations will still be the migration routes between deep water and spawning areas, although bass will be continually moving shallower. In reservoirs, look at the shallow flats close to major creek channels. In natural lakes, shallow bays and coves are the best choice. Analyze the body of water you will be fishing and figure out where those fish are going to spawn. Look for protected spawning areas in your given body of water—whether pond, lake, or reservoir. If it's a river, maybe find little pockets out

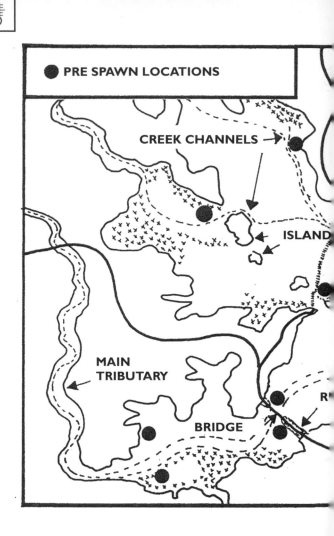

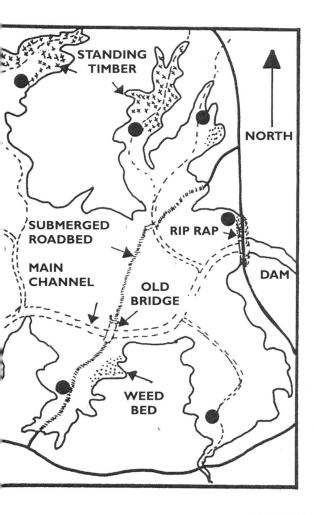

STANDING TIMBER

NORTH

SUBMERGED ROADBED

RIP RAP

MAIN CHANNEL

DAM

OLD BRIDGE

WEED BED

of the current. If a lake, maybe consider one of those flat coves or a little pocket off a cove. Then look for isolated targets near those areas. Usually the larger fish like to get up against something. Also try to find off-colored water.

In the shallower lakes, like river impoundments, the fish will generally be shallower and seek cover in wood or some wood-oriented structure unless the impoundment has weeds. If weeds are present, they will always be the predominant pre-spawn cover used by fish, especially big females. Quite often anglers cast away from the biggest pre-spawn bass. Early in the year, anglers often begin casting at the shoreline. Usually they catch early male bass—one- to three-pound fish. Most of the big females are behind them, usually along or over the top of the outer edge of the weeds, or on semi-shallow stick-ups and brush. One tactic that has worked for me is to look

for near-shore areas with good cover and a bottom composed of pea gravel, with maybe some scattered rock chunks or sand—places where fish are likely to make their spawning beds. Then go to the nearest tributary and fish the first and adjacent point. Even when the first group of bass are actually on the spawning beds, there are plenty of five-, six-, and seven-pound bass on these secondary points—often subtle pieces of structure—just outside the spawning areas.

Best action occurs when the water temperature stabilizes above 55 degrees F, which usually occurs once the nights, as well as the days, start becoming warm. When bass move onto these spawning areas just preparatory to the actual spawn, the action is the best of any time of the year.

Not all bass in a lake spawn at the same time, however, and if you wish to have a long pre-spawn season, merely follow the rising water temperature backward. For instance, you started in the early spring on the north side of the lake in the coves against the south-facing shore. When these areas warm to the point the bass are spawning in these areas, move to the southern shore facing the north.

Some bass also live and spawn in the middle of the lake in reservoirs and lakes with good mid-lake cover. These bass will normally be the last to spawn. This is particularly so on Truman, a lake near my home in Missouri. It's not uncommon to see bass spawning in the treetops on underwater islands, humps, and other structure such as old roadbeds, and so forth, even into early summer.

Pre-spawn bass are located relatively shallow compared to their deep water, early-spring haunts. Look from extremely shallow 1 to 2 feet down, to 6 to 8 feet, depending on clarity and amount of cover. If cold fronts occur, back up to the closest deeper water.

On lakes with willows, or lakes that have flooded brush from spring rains, the fish will show up along the outer edge of the brush first and then as spawning draws closer, move farther back into the brush where they're harder to catch. Pick a key feature, such as a lone bush, the tip or side of a point, or a secondary point with brush that sticks out farther than other brush. These are typical of the first places fish will appear before they begin scattering en route to their nesting sites.

Pre-spawn bass are basically feeding fish. They're filling their bellies, and their metabolism is increasing because the water is warming up. Large bass move to the shallows at this time of the year, even if it is a month or so before they spawn. Most of the food at that time of the year is in the shallow cover, the grass line edges, or a tree line that intersects the shore. Bass follow a certain route toward the shore, and the difference at that time of the year is they don't retire back to deep-water sanctuaries.

Lure Choices

Although pig-and-jig can still be productive, locator lures that are retrieved at a faster pace to search for roaming bass are

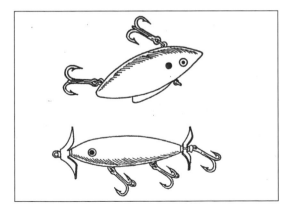

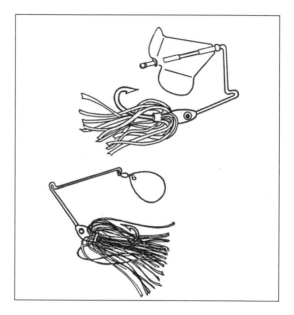

the best choice. These include: spinner-baits, crankbaits, jerkbaits, and topwater lures or buzzbaits.

Tactics

Even these faster-moving lures should be used fairly slowly at the start of this peri-

Use fast-moving lures such as spinnerbaits, buzzbaits, shallow crankbaits, and topwaters to prospect as much water as possible. Switch to slower baits on short strikers.

od, increasing the retrieval speed as the water continues to warm. One tactic is to explore with these lures, and if you get a strike but don't hook the bass, switch to a slower lure such as pig-and-jig or plastic worm and rework the area. Or you can simply slow down your retrieve with the

One of my all-time-favorite lures for this season is a Rat-L-Trap.

spinnerbait or crankbait. If you get several short strikes with a buzzbait, try using a stinger or back hook. Crawfish are one of the most common food sources at this time of the year, and one of the best imitators is a jig with a crawfish trailer. One of my favorites is a big-lipped, deep-diving crankbait bounced off the rocks and timber. An old-time Arbogast MudBug with the big metal lip caught my biggest stringer of big pre-spawn bass. But, my all-time-favorite search-and-destroy is a

A big, metal-lipped Arbogast MudBug is another favorite.

Rat-L-Trap. Another search-type lure that has gained popularity is the Umbrella Rig, but make sure you follow the number of hooks allowed by your state.

Despite the opportunities for big bass, the pre-spawn period can be frustrating. Spring rains often bring an influx of water with a lot of dirty water coming in. And there are the cold fronts. A searching pattern, such as when using spinnerbaits, may slow down because the fish get tighter to cover under these conditions, and then the jig bite starts. You need to pay a lot of attention to the weather conditions at that time of year. The more stable it is, the more baits that come into play. The more adverse it is, the more you are going to have to drop back to one or two baits— maybe flipping a jig tight to cover. Or it may be slow rolling a spinnerbait over some grass—or through whatever cover exists.

The smaller males spend more time in the shallows than the bigger females. If you're continually catching small fish, back out to deeper water.

Small Waters

This is also a great time to prospect small waters such as community lakes, strip pits, and farm ponds. Numerous old strip pits surrounded the farm I grew up on, and I unfortunately spent more time exploring them and pursuing the big bass they grew

Small waters such as ponds, community lakes, and mining pits also offer great black bass fishing.

than pursuing my school lessons. After more years of chasing bass around the countryside from major reservoir to major reservoir and more pounding boat rides than I care to remember, I still enjoy the quiet small waters of pits and farm ponds. And more than once I took a fishing rod to golf-course ponds when on assignment testing boats in some locales. Many farm ponds, small city water supply lakes, state parks, state managed lakes, and even some streams offer excellent bank fishing opportunities.

This is basic bass fishing; all that's needed is a rod, lures, and a stringer if you're planning to keep a bass or two for the skillet. There's no reason to carry a big tackle box, and in fact, that can slow you down. A small waist-held tackle box or pack will tote everything. If you wish to boat to bass, a canoe, small jon boat, or plastic bassin' rig works well. Tackle should be matched to the situation, depending on water clarity and amount of vegetation. For the most part it pays to downscale equipment in many smaller waters, depending on the situation. For farm ponds and strip pits with extremely clear water, 8- to 10-pound test line on medium weight spinning gear or your favorite casting rod is a good choice. For larger city lakes or water with stained or off-color water, or a lot of cover and stumps, you may wish to move up to 17- to 20-pound test.

Downsizing lures is also more productive on extremely clear waters. Also always match the lure to the forage fish commonly found, which for the most part includes bluegill or sun perch, crawdads, frogs, and even small catfish. Many of the old-timers work well, and my all-time three favorites are a Hula Popper, Bass Oreno, and Smithwick

Devil's Horse. Of course standards such as spinnerbaits, spinner jigs, and plastic worms are great. If there's a lot of moss and vegetation, rubber frogs can be the ticket. A pig-and-jig is also extremely effective at times.

Timing
These small waters tend to warm up somewhat quicker in the spring, and when fishing them you should use the basic seasonal approach in tactics as for the bigger waters. Pre-spawn, however, again is the single best time to catch a big lunker bass from small waters.

This is the time of year you can catch your biggest bass.

Even wade-fishing can be successful.

Spinnerbaits also work great at this time of the year.

SPAWN:
Late April/May

Temperature: 65 to 75 degrees F
Clarity: Turbid to clear
Water Conditions: Normally stable with occasional influx

Normally the water temperature will range from 65 to 75 degrees F while clarity will run from turbid to clear, depending on lake location and the amount of runoff. Fairly warm weather has stabilized, and most of the early-spring runoff has slowed down. This can be both a tough and easy period, depending on the exact timing of your fishing. The chances of catching big bass are quite good, but you'll probably have to work fairly hard for them.

Bass Locations

Locating good spawning areas is actually a key to consistently successful bass fishing on a year-round basis. Not just to fish the spawning areas, but because bass

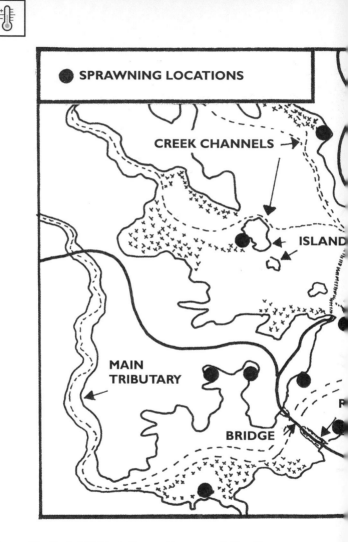

SPRAWNING LOCATIONS

CREEK CHANNELS →

ISLAND

MAIN
TRIBUTARY

BRIDGE

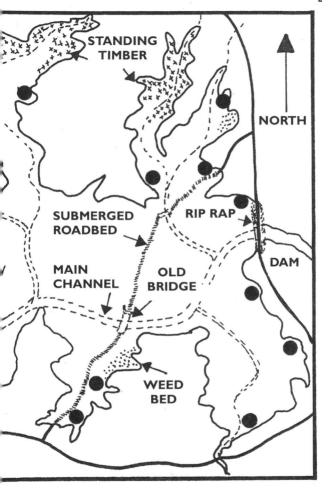

STANDING TIMBER

NORTH

SUBMERGED ROADBED

RIP RAP

DAM

MAIN CHANNEL

OLD BRIDGE

WEED BED

relate to these specific areas throughout the rest of the year.

Good spawning locations can vary a great deal from lake to lake depending on the structure, but all have three requirements. First, a fairly solid bottom, such as gravel, small rocks, and so forth. Soft, mucky, weedy areas are rarely chosen unless the fish can clean down to a solid bottom to create a bed. Depth is second and will be fairly shallow, providing plenty of sunlight to incubate the eggs. Depth will range from a foot to 8 to 10 feet deep, depending on water clarity, structure, and so forth. Third, there should be little or no current to wash eggs away. Most of these areas will also be located fairly close to deep water, such as submerged channels.

Lure Choices

Plastic worms, tube lures, swimbaits, and topwater lures such as Zara Spooks are

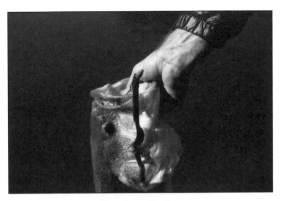

Plastic worm is an excellent choice for the spawn.

good. The single most productive lure at this time is a plastic salamander.

Tactics

Many serious bass anglers do not fish for spawning bass, but follow the gradual pre-spawn cycle mentioned earlier. This is for two reasons: first, spawning bass do not feed, although you can sometimes trick them into striking. If you're fishing a tournament, it's best to look for bass that are

The top choice, however, is a plastic salamander.

still in a pre-spawn period. The second reason is conservation. Although fishing for spawning bass is legal in many states, removing nesting bass from a heavily pressured reservoir or lake can have negative effects.

In most instances you'll usually catch the small males guarding the nest. Plastic worms and salamanders tossed time and again into or over a nest can, however,

Gitzits and tube lures can be quite productive for spawning bass. Sight cast directly into nests.

often provoke nesting bass to hit. Gitzits and tube lures can also be quite productive when sight cast directly into nests. Big bass will often take these lures by the tail or tip and attempt to carry them off the nest.

Temperature: 75 to 80 degrees F
Clarity: Clear
Water Conditions: Stable

Temperatures will range from 75 to 80 degrees F and up. Clarity will quite often be clear to extremely clear, although occasionally runoff may produce some turbidity. Windy weather can also create some turbid conditions on shallow lakes.

As mentioned earlier, all bass don't spawn at the same time, and many anglers prefer to fish for the active fish, such as pre-spawners, in other parts of the lake, or look for the summer pattern of the early spawners.

Bass Locations

Once the spawn is over, a majority of the bass, particularly the males, retreat to the nearest deeper water to recuperate. Look basically at the nearby migration

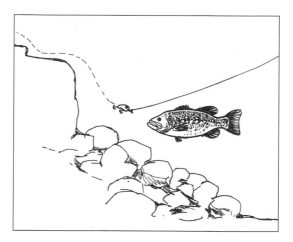

Medium to deep-diving crankbaits used on migration routes and underwater structure between spawning areas and deep water can be productive. Begin using plastic worms, Gitzits, and grubs on deep structure.

routes between the spawning area and deep water, starting shallow and working your way outward until you discover fish. Key areas are the deeper ends of major lake points, creek channels, and so forth. Depth will be anywhere from 8 to 20 feet.

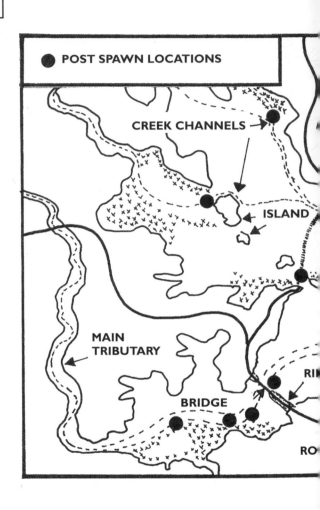

POST SPAWN LOCATIONS

CREEK CHANNELS

ISLAND

MAIN TRIBUTARY

BRIDGE

RI...

RO...

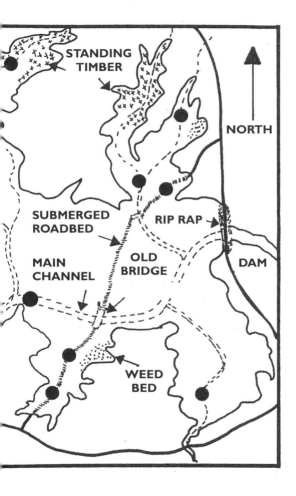

STANDING TIMBER

NORTH

SUBMERGED ROADBED

RIP RAP

MAIN CHANNEL

OLD BRIDGE

DAM

WEED BED

Lure Choices

Extremely slow-working lures such as pig-and-jig, plastic worms, grubs, and tube lures are the usual choice. Crankbaits bumped along the bottom in a medium to slow retrieve will also help locate bass. Spinnerbaits, pumped slowly and dropped back to the bottom, are also good choices.

Tactics

This can be a tough time of the year, simply because many bass have become inactive. Unfortunately, it's also the time many anglers take their annual vacations.

The main key is to stay as versatile as possible. Try different lures and patterns, and prospect until you find active fish. Early in the day and late in the evening often provide the best angling during this time period.

Again, follow the main migration routes, this time backward toward deeper summer-

Follow the migration routes back to deeper water.

water holding areas that can be productive. Start at or near spawning areas and simply work backwards toward deeper water.

SUMMER:
July/August

Temperature: 80 degrees F and up
Clarity: Clear
Water Conditions: Stable

The surface layer will be hot—80 degrees F and up. Water clarity will vary, according to local conditions, from extremely clear to occasionally turbid.

Depth varies greatly according to water clarity, the lake thermocline level, structure, and cover. Basically there are two summertime patterns, depending on the type of lake: shallow or deep. Some lakes may only have one pattern, deep or shallow, while both patterns may exist in other lakes.

Bass Locations

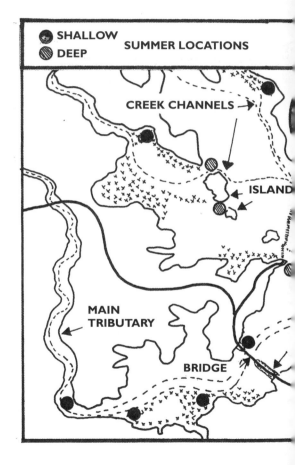

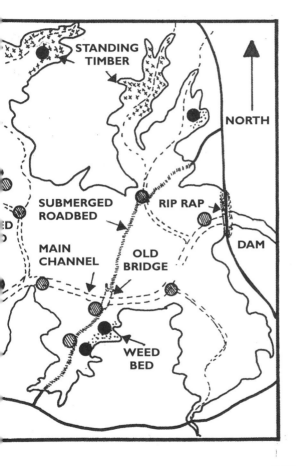

STANDING
TIMBER

NORTH

SUBMERGED
ROADBED

RIP RAP

MAIN
CHANNEL

OLD
BRIDGE

DAM

WEED
BED

Shallow: Look for cover in the way of vegetation such as weeds, moss, overhanging trees, submerged brush, and stump beds. Boat docks are a favorite hangout on many lakes.

Deep: Look for sloping main lake points, humps, islands, underwater springs, and deep-water structure such as old bridges, roads, submerged buildings, and so forth.

Note: Headwaters or main tributaries of lakes and reservoirs are always top producers during summer months. These areas often provide both shallow and

On shallow lakes look for cover.

On deeper lakes look for structure.

deep water in one small area. They are also usually more oxygenated due to inflowing water. Water temperature may also be somewhat cooler.

Tactics

Again, tactics vary according to depth. For shallow water, early morning, late evening, and night fishing are the best, particularly on clear-water lakes. Plastic worms, dark colored spinnerbaits, or topwater lures and buzzbaits are top nighttime producers.

Minnow baits, jerkbaits, and swimbaits twitched or retrieved slowly are often good producers during summertime. An extremely popular summer lure is a swim-bait. These come in either a soft solid or hollow body to which you add a weighted hook, as well as pre-rigged soft and hard bodies. They're also available in a wide variety of sizes and colors. Swimbaits can actually be used year-round, but they tend

Depending on temperature and weather conditions, late evening and early morning are the best fishing periods.

to shine in clear water, and can be used shallow or deep as they'll draw fish for some distance.

Weighted-hook soft plastic swimbaits are the best choice for shallow water. Look for stumps, brush, and other woody cover, cast past the cover, then retrieve slowly. This is also a great tactic for boat docks. Some anglers prefer to twitch the lure occasionally, making it change directions, providing even more enticement for big bass.

Both weighted hook, and the heavier solid-body, pre-rigged swimbaits can be used for deeper water. You'll need a heavier weighted lure, and solid-body, pre-rigged models are usually the best choice. When fishing deep-water structure such as points or humps, fish from the uphill side, casting over to the deeper side and bringing the swimbait up to the shallower water.

The plastic worm can be rigged in several ways, and Texas-style, wacky, and "do-nothing" are top choices. The venerable Texas-style is the most popular, either using loose weights or pegging the weight in place. For summer fishing for big bass, try a giant 12-inch worm. Although I fished with the first Creme plastic worms, these days a wide variety of worm styles, sizes, and colors are available. Hooks are also available in a wide variety of styles and sizes. Brass-style Texas rigging is another variety utilizing brass weights, brass tickers, and glass beads to produce more sound. Carolina rigging is also extremely popular in some situations and has grown with the increased use of brass weights and glass beads. An extremely productive fishing rig that allows quicker coverage of more water with plastic worms, the rig consists of a brass sliding weight, a glass bead, then a swivel, and finally a

The plastic worm is the number one choice for many summer anglers.

3- to 6-foot leader usually with a plastic worm or salamander rigged with the hook buried in the body Texas-style. The affair is lobbed out, then brought back in a fairly fast lift-and-drop retrieve. The worm tends to float off the bottom while the weight system bangs along stirring up the bottom and making nose.

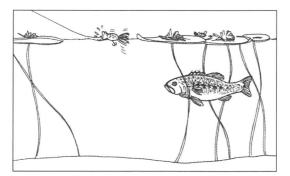

For deep-water bass, small grubs, worms, and tube lures jigged vertically over schools of bass are a producer on sultry hot days. Tube jigs are also great for fishing around bridge piers and under docks.

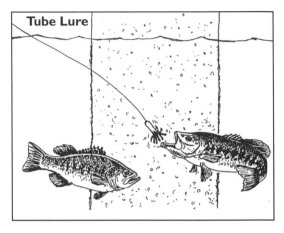

Tube Lure

Tube lures and jigs and grubs are great choices for pitching around underwater structure, including bridge piers.

Jigging spoons vertically jigged over underwater humps can produce, although you'll often have to fight other species off. Crankbaits suited to summer forage-size fish brought across points, humps, and other structure, or bumped off woody cover, can produce. Spinnerbaits retrieved deep along bluffs work in some areas. By the same token, pig-and-jigs bounced

Crankbaits brought across underwater humps, long points, and areas with stump beds can be productive.

over deep-water structure can also be extremely productive.

Night Fishing

Nighttime fishing can provide some of the most exciting and rewarding bass fishing, particularly during the summer months when boaters and recreationists swarm

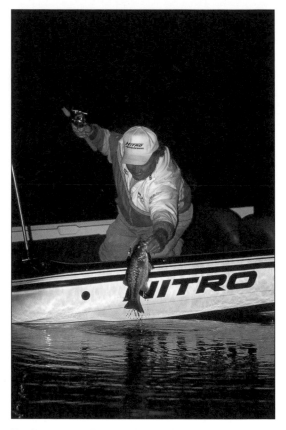

Your best summer choice may be night fishing.

the lake, and the scorching sun makes it too hot to enjoy day fishing. Experienced night prowlers first find fish, or find daytime locations that hold fish, then look for where those fish will go after dark. In many reservoirs bass have a tendency to hang out during the day on the old creek banks, especially those with submerged pole timber or stumps. When it gets dark they move up on the flats and banks to chase shad and eat crawdads. Another good spot is a pea gravel or sloping point that runs out from the bank and drops off into the creek channel, another typical but short migration route. Using a lake map, locate places where the creek channel sweeps in close to bank. Then scout the area in daylight before you head out for a night fishing trip. Other nighttime choices include long main-lake points, humps, and underwater islands, especially those near creek or river channels. The most productive of these will have stumps, cedar or tree rows, standing or submerged timber or rock piles. Riprap along bridge causeways and dam faces are also excellent nighttime prospecting spots, as is one quite unusual pattern, swimming beaches. In many reservoirs when the last swimmers leave, bass move up on these man-made beaches because the baitfish move in to feed on the algae stirred up by swimmers.

Although bass may hit topwater lures right at dusk, the best fishing usually doesn't start until later in the night, usually around 10 to 11 o'clock. The fish will usually bite well until the sun comes up. Some anglers like a full moon, others prefer the dark of the moon.

Lures

Plastic worms, jig-and-frog or eel, buzzbaits, and spinnerbaits are all popular night bassing lures. Big plastic worms tossed alongside exposed pole timber and allowed to drop down are great. When bass are actively chasing bait, a Jitterbug, Rat-L-Trap, or Zara Spook can not only be productive but a lot of fun as well. With worms or pig-and-jig, it's important to stay in contact with the bottom as much as possible.

Tactics

One tactic on some reservoirs is to fish with a live crawfish, a great tactic for smallmouth and Kentuckies. Use a No. 2 Tru-Turn hook through the crawfish tail and a ¼-ounce split shot about 6 inches above the crawfish.

Some anglers utilize black light and fluorescent line to increase hookset because you can see your line. A lot of times bass will pick up a lure such as a plastic worm and run to the side or even toward

Fishing the deep underwater humps in the summer can result in some fantastic smallmouth fishing.

you. They can drop the bait before you even know it, if you're not watching your line. You can catch a lot of smallmouth and Kentuckies at night.

A great late summer tactic in lakes with good smallmouth populations in both the northern and southern United States is fishing the underwater humps. I've found this good on Rainy Lake in Minnesota, Lake Erie, and Stockton Lake in Missouri near my home. The depth varies. In some areas, such as Rainy Lake, this may be 70 to 80 feet. On Stockton, depth may range from 15 to 25 feet. The depth of the thermocline determines the depth. The humps must have rocks or rubble right on the drop or edge. Jigs with plastic trailers are great, but so is live bait, including a Lindy Rig, or horse-head jig. Baits include nightcrawlers and crawfish.

Temperature: 80 to 60 degrees F
Clarity: Clear to turbid
Water Conditions: Sometimes rising

Cooling fall weather will start bringing surface water temperatures down from 80 to around 60 degrees F. Although some lakes may have ultra-clear water at this time, others will have quite turbid areas as fall rains bring floodwaters into the lake. This flushes the lake as well as creates rising water levels. Fall turnover may occur during the latter part of this period and can have an effect at this time as well. Summer vegetation die-off occurs.

Actually the fall season can be broken down into three distinct periods: early fall, mid-fall and late fall. Early fall occurs with the first cooling down period. Mid-fall contains the turnover as the lake water temperature equalizes from the layered summer temperatures, and late fall occurs

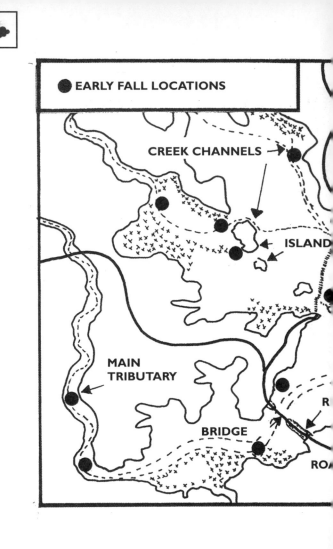

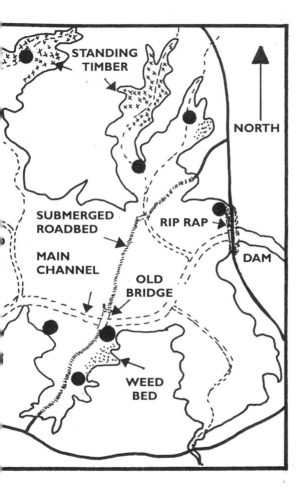

after the turnover as the water temperature continues to drop. These can occur in a short time span or over several weeks, depending on local temperatures, weather, and water conditions.

Bass Locations

During the first part of the fall season bass will be in the same place as their summer holding areas, although moving around more and on the migration route between the deep and shallow water areas. As the water and air temperature start to drop, bass will move toward the shallow areas and spend more time feeding. A sudden water rise due to fall rains can cause a mass migration into the freshly submerged weeds and brush. Major tributaries are also prime fall spots as forage fish move up into these areas following the influx of water and bass follow them. Depth varies from shallow to deep, or just above the thermocline.

Lure Choices

Spinnerbaits, buzzbaits, and crankbaits are top choices at this time, as are umbrella rigs. Zara Spooks or other topwater lures can be extremely good when worked in submerged trees, over major channels, or over deteriorating weed beds. Shallow running crankbaits or rattling shad–type baits are also excellent for this pattern.

Spinnerbaits are one of the top choices at this time.

Tactics

Since bass are moving more, more spread out, as well as more aggressive, retrieves should be fairly fast and in searching patterns. Lures should be larger sized at this time to match the larger size of the forage. Shad are the top forage on many reservoirs and lakes, and anything white or silver can be productive. This is one of those periods when you can literally load a boat with bass.

In some ways this is a backward migration. During the dog days of summer, as August is often called, the majority of the shad, the main bass forage of many reservoirs, roam the open deeper water. Bass typically are in their deeper water summer haunts, frequenting shallow water only during night or occasionally in daytime low-light periods. Once the temperature drops from the summer high into the sixties, huge schools of shad

Shad-shaped crankbaits, jerkbaits, and swimbaits fished in the tributaries are extremely productive.

begin to form and head for the shallows and especially up into the creeks and tributaries. Typically fall rains flush new water into these areas, adding even more plankton and food for shad and minnows. Bass that have followed the forage out into the main lake during the summer months follow these huge schools of shad back up into the shallows—the coves, flats, creeks, creek arms, and rivers—in a feeding frenzy before the cold onset of winter. Knowing how to locate and follow this fall forage, then matching the forage with the correct lure and action, can result in extremely successful bass fishing.

The first step is map work. Look for a main tributary, or an area with several tributaries, to prospect. Even small creeks can offer good bassing. Once you've determined that a creek or tributary looks promising, start at the mouth and do a little electronics scouting. First, scout the underwater juncture where the creek meets the main tributary feeding the lake, or the mouth of the main tributary where it comes into the lake. If the bass haven't begun their shallow water migration, they may still be located in these summer holding spots. Look for schools of suspended shad. Then move to the main lake points on either side of the creek or tributary mouth and again look for bait schools. Start on the deep end of the point and work shallower. Then simply work your way upstream, checking each secondary point as well as the inundated creek or river channel for baitfish. Often you'll locate a concentration of baitfish and bass at the first spot the channel is no longer inundated but follows its natural banks. It's just a matter of starting at the mouth and working back until you locate baitfish and bass. If you don't find shad, look for another creek.

Temperature: 60 to 42 degrees F
Clarity: Turbid
Water Conditions: Rising

Water temperatures continue to drop from 60 to 42 degrees F. Water is usually fairly turbid due to incoming rainwater as well as lake turnover. Conditions will become more stable in the latter part of the period. This is also an extremely good time to be bass fishing almost any-where. In fact, those that forgo hunting for bass fishing often have the best fishing days of the year. Dress warmly and adjust lures and tactics as the season progresses.

As the lake continues to cool, bass become more active in their need to fill up before the coming winter months. Bass can be located almost any place at this time, but shallow water areas, particularly those close to major migration routes, can all be productive. The fish are moving back to their winter holding areas and the same places you found success in early spring can again be productive. The upper ends of tributaries and major creeks can be extremely productive, as they provide shallow-water migration routes, and deep water in a relatively small area. Depth varies from 1 to 12 feet.

Lure Choices

Spinnerbaits, crankbaits, and buzzbaits are all good choices, because they're fast-moving prospecting baits and bass are feeding aggressively. As the water temperature continues to drop, slow down your tactics, and pig-and-jig can become increasingly more productive.

Tactics

Fishing tactics should be fairly slow during the annual fall turnover. While this

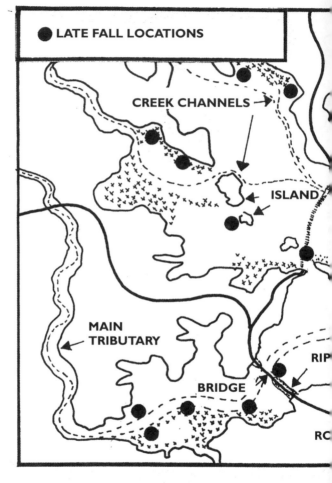

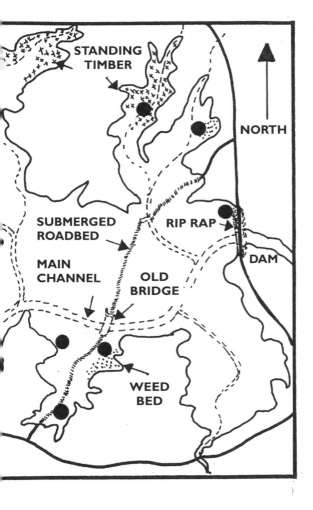

STANDING TIMBER

NORTH

SUBMERGED ROADBED

RIP RAP

DAM

MAIN CHANNEL

OLD BRIDGE

WEED BED

annual phenomenon is going on, fishing can be really tough because the bass are disoriented. Once this is over and there is a fresh mix of oxygenated water throughout the lake, fishing can be the best it's been since early spring. Retrieves should be sped up to garner strikes from aggressive fish and also to cover a lot of territory. As the weather gets progressively colder, fish tend to drop back deeper and become less aggressive; however, a warming day or two can bring on renewed activity, and spinnerbaits and crankbaits are hard to beat at that time.

During this period, bass are actively moving chasing bait and feeding up for the winter.

Temperature: 43 to 45 degrees F
Clarity: Clear
Water Conditions: Stable

Water temperatures will be 45 degrees F and colder over most of the country, except the deep south. Some lakes may also freeze over. Water is usually fairly clear. Winter provides some excellent bass fishing for those willing to dress and prepare for the cold weather.

Bass Locations

Most bass will be schooled in deep-water holding areas at this time, although they may make occasional forays into shallow water along major migration routes. Winter bass prefer vertical holding areas such as bluffs, submerged trees, and deep creek channels, rather than the sloping areas of shallows and flats. The reason is they can "migrate" vertically simply

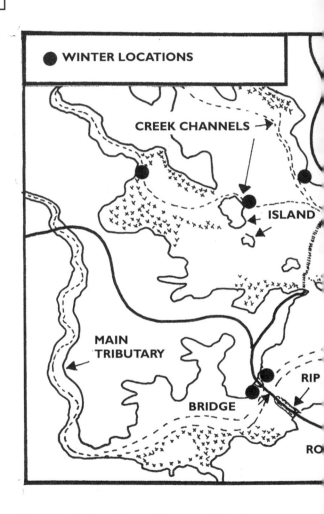

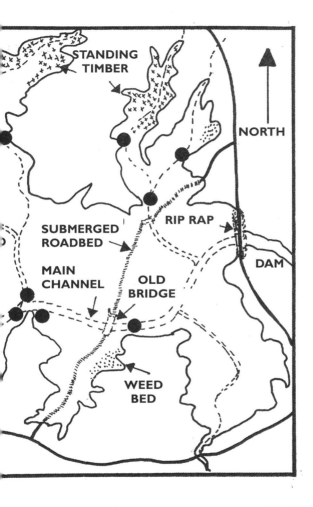

STANDING
TIMBER

NORTH

SUBMERGED
ROADBED

RIP RAP

DAM

MAIN
CHANNEL

OLD
BRIDGE

WEED
BED

by ascending or descending, rather than making a horizontal migration for food or body temperature adjustment.

Depth varies according to structure, surface water temperature, and water clarity but is usually 18 to 30 feet or deeper, although bass will move shallow during warm spells.

Lure Choices
Pig-and-jig or almost any type of jig with a plastic trailer is good. Jigging spoons, spinnerbaits, and modified jerkbaits as described in early spring work as well.

Tactics
Start medium shallow and gradually work deeper until you locate the fish. Fish the vertical areas such as submerged timber, bluffs, and so forth. Look for bass suspended in any of these areas, or just off the edges or drops of the creek channels. A

Weight jerkbaits to suspend and jerk through drowned treetops, or vertical fish with jigging spoons for winter bass.

pig-and-jig can be bounced slowly down a bluff wall until you locate the depth fish are holding. Then fish similar structures at that depth. A jigging spoon fished vertically in the treetops for suspended bass is especially good on sunny days. Jerkbaits that have been modified to be weighted to make them neutral buoyant can be cranked down to suspended bass then stopped. Slow rolling spinnerbaits along bluff faces is also a good tactic.

GETTING AND KEEPING LIVE BAITS

One of my dad's favorite fishing tactics was to put a big minnow below a big cork and, using his cane pole, fish the strip pits near our home for largemouth bass, and I mean big bass. My favorite thing was first, our visit to the creek to seine minnows for bait.

Most bass these days are caught on artificial lures, but bass will readily take any number of live baits, and although they are not allowed for tournament fishing, live baits can often save the day. Actually there's probably nothing that swims, crawls, or flies that bass won't eat, including minnows, goldfish, crawfish, frogs, snakes, worms, and other fish, including smaller bass. If you want to use live bait for bass, having the bait you need at the right time is an important facet of live bait

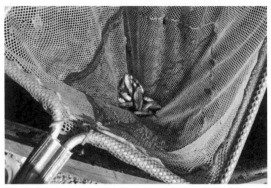

Keeping minnows and other live baits can provide baits when you need them.

bass angling, and keeping bait can be even more invaluable.

Minnows

Minnows are a good choice for bass, but not just any minnow may be effective. Depending on locale, bass may show a preference to specific minnow species. Fathead minnows are the hardiest and will normally stay lively longer than the chubs or shiners. You may, however, be limited to what you can purchase in your local area. If you have access to a small creek, you can use a minnow trap or even a seine to acquire minnows. For the most part, however, these will be chubs or shiners.

Regardless of how you get them, minnows left at the end of the day can present a problem, as can getting minnows early in the morning. Serious minnow dunkers go through a good amount of bait in a season's time. Keeping minnows at home

Minnows, crawfish, and other live baits can often by trapped with a minnow trap.

can cut down on the cost and provide a reliable supply of bait when you want it. Many products are now available, including tanks, aerators, and water treatment chemicals, that aid in keeping minnows frisky and healthy. You can keep a limited number of minnows alive with a DC- or battery-powered aerator, and some aerator units can be placed in any container. A big insulated cooler makes a good "minnow tank." A 110V-system can also be set up to keep bait indefinitely. A number of aerators for use in tanks are available, as are tanks and/or complete units. The electric supply must be protected by a ground-fault interrupter.

My system consists of a Rubbermaid 60-gallon stock tank with a 110V-aerator. This is a quite simple system, but it can also be improved with a bit of effort. In order to support the agitator and also to keep the bait quiet and prevent algae

An aerated bait tank can be used to hold any number of live baits. The tank shown utilizes 110V-aerator with a plastic stock tank.

growth from light, make a lid of ⅜-inch treated plywood, with a hinged lift-up section. Actually the lid is in three sections, and I divided the tank in half to keep minnows of two different sizes. A piece of treated plywood with a center hole cut out and galvanized screen wire fastened over the hole is the divider. It's fastened to a cleat on the underside of the center top piece which is anchored solidly to the tank top. Lids on both sides are hinged to the center strip. This works quite well, but you can improve the keeping ability by adding an overflow drain tube and an intake attached to a garden hose. It doesn't take much, just a trickle of fresh water will maintain livelier bait. The tank should be placed in a cool dark spot in your garage or shed.

Several tactics can also help keep baits longer. First, remove all dead bait immediately. Check your tank morning and

Purchased aerating systems can also be used for home storage of baits.

evening and remove any dead minnows. Limit handling of all bait as much as possible, and then handle them gently. Rock salt (approximately 1½ cups per 26 gallons) can be added each time you fill the tank to help keep scales intact. Rinse agitator and tank thoroughly after each use to reduce harmful bacteria and algae. Minnows can be transported in minnow buckets, aerated minnow buckets or live wells. Aerated minnow buckets are the best choice.

Goldfish and Other Fish Species

One extremely effective fishing tactic in Florida is using big shiners or even goldfish for big bass by floating them under a big cork, just as my dad did. And it will work just about anywhere else as well. Shiners and goldfish are often sold at bait shops catering to big cat anglers. They are

A variety of minnow buckets are available for holding baits while fishing.

fairly easy to keep in the same set-up as described for minnows. Other fish species, such as bluegill and perch, can also be effective, but check state game laws regarding their use. These can also be kept in the minnow set-up.

Nightcrawlers

Earthworms, or nightcrawlers, can also be extremely effective, but the biggest problem is keeping the other fish species, such as bluegill and perch, as well as catfish, from stealing them off your hook. But that's a good problem; simply catch what takes your bait. One of my favorite tactics for walleye is dragging a nightcrawler on a bottom bouncer rig, and in areas where bass are available, I catch as many bass as walleye. Nightcrawlers are available almost anywhere including many quick-stop stations and even in grocery stores in some locales. But there are crawlers and there are crawlers. The best crawlers are fat and sassy. Ordinary garden worms can also be used, but they're smaller and usually not as "active" in attracting bass.

You can also collect your own crawlers. The best time is after a long, soaking nighttime rain. As the rain saturates the soil, it drives the crawlers up to the surface. You can oftentimes simply pick a good number off your driveway, on the sidewalks, and I sometimes even find

Earthworms and nightcrawlers can be kept using a variety of products available.

them in my garage. If the rain stops in the night, you can quite often collect night-crawlers with a flashlight with a red lens in short-cropped grass areas. Folks have invented many different tactics and products for collecting worms. Some utilize a battery-powered unit that stimulates worms and drives them to the surface. One old-fashioned method is "fiddling up" worms. A notched stick is driven into the ground and another stick rubbed up and down the notches to create a vibration to bring worms to the surface. A potato fork driven into the ground and struck with another object also sometimes works.

Keeping earthworms is fairly easy, and growing a supply is also fairly easy. Growing nightcrawlers takes a bit more effort, but keeping them is, again, fairly easy. Simply keep them in a Styrofoam box in a refrigerator. You can keep a good quantity in this manner, and when you head to the lake simply take a small Styrofoam cooler with a day's supply. A small ice pack in the cooler will help keep the worms throughout the day, especially if the day is hot. Some anglers like to condition their worms the night before by placing them between ice-cold layers of wet newspaper, or you can simply toss them in a container of ice water the night before. They will be fat and wiggly.

You can easily raise garden worms, or purchased "red wigglers," but raising nightcrawlers takes a great deal more expertise and work. You'll need a container to hold the worms (a large old cooler is a good choice), but you must drill a few small holes in the top for ventilation. Fill the container with a good garden soil that is not sandy. Thoroughly mix in one cup of dry dog food and sprinkle about a quart of water over the soil. Place twenty-five to fifty earthworms on top of the soil. Dampen a couple of sheets of newspaper and place over the worms.

Place the worm box in a cool part of your basement, away from the furnace, but where the temperature will stay 60 to 75 degrees Fahrenheit. Temperature is very important. If the temperature rises much above 70 degrees, the worms may die; if the temperature drops below 60 degrees, reproduction may be slowed. Use an inexpensive thermometer to monitor the soil temperature.

Inspect your worm box once a week. If the surface is dry add a little water, but don't overwater. If the soil is muddy, you're overfeeding and overwatering. About every three weeks remove the top two or three inches of soil and mix in one-half cup of dry dog food. Dump the remainder of the soil out and check on your worm "herd." Place the newly fed soil in the bottom of the container and replace the rest of the soil and the worms. In six to eight weeks you should have a new crop of worms. And if you're a good worm farmer, you can expect from seven hundred to a thousand worms.

Raising nightcrawlers, however, is a bit trickier. They require a bedding temperature of 40 to 50 degrees Fahrenheit. You can keep a large supply, however, over a long period of time if you have a refrigerator and a worm box that fits inside it. Quite frankly, if you're going to try raising nightcrawlers, your best bet is the Magic Products worm bedding.

Crawfish

At times, nothing beats crawfish, especially for smallmouth bass, and that is the reason so many artificial baits are designed to resemble crawfish. These include hard baits and the extremely popular jig and plastic craw. Crawfish can sometimes be purchased at bait shops, but a minnow trap is all that's required. Bait with stale, hard bread to catch minnows, bait with canned cat food to catch crawfish. Just punch holes in the cat food can and put the whole can in the trap.

Crawfish are fairly easy to keep as well. Use an aerated bait tank with a cage partially suspended above water so they can occasionally crawl out in the air. A minnow trap works well for this. To keep them frisky and healthy during fishing or while transporting, keep them in an insulated foam bait bucket with a handful of dampened grass or moss.

A variety of bait-gathering products are available.

ABOUT THE AUTHOR

Monte Burch grew up fishing for largemouth bass in the numerous strip pits and farm ponds surrounding his parents' farm in central Missouri and today lives close at hand to popular bass lakes such as Truman, Stockton, Table Rock, and Pomme de Terre in central Missouri.

Monte has been writing about largemouth bass fishing for half a century. He has followed many of the major tournament trails, including a number of B.A.S.S. Classics and fished all across North America. Once a staffer for *Bass Times*, he has been a contributor to many national magazines such as *Sports Afield*, *Bassmaster*, *U.S. Bass*, *In-Fisherman*, *North American Fisherman*, and many others.

NOTES

NOTES